THE LESS SAID

a collection of short-form poetry

GAIL HARTMAN
ANN REED
KATE TUCKER

ISBN: 978-0-9654862-2-4

Published by Turtlecub Productions
Minneapolis, MN

Contents

Introduction

Greetings, dear Reader, from the three of us. We are friends who write, and we are writers who are friends. We are a psychotherapist, singer-songwriter, and a minister who love the shape and sound and power of words. If you like, you can read more about us in the final pages of this book in the section entitled **More Said**.

Several years ago we began meeting regularly, to share what we're writing, to talk about our process, to commiserate when we're feeling stuck, and to explore the practices that help us keep the pen in our hand, or our fingers on the keyboard.

Then, in summer 2019, Gail and Ann (longtime haiku writers) had an idea. They made a list of thirteen short poetry forms (see list at the end of the introduction) and said: what if, starting now, we all write one little poem each day. On day #1, we'll each write a **Nonet** and text it to each other. On day #2, we'll each write a **Butterfly Cinquain**, and (again) text it to each other. We'll continue down the list of forms, and after thirteen days, we'll start again at the top.

This will be fun, we thought, and an interesting discipline. The counting of lines and syllables will occupy the finicky part our minds. It will be just enough structure to get past the inner critic and set us free. We won't overthink. We'll simply write, and share what we write.

That was July 2019. We were true to our plan and wrote many, many poems — poems which served as exercises in verbal economy, as tiny journal entries, and as another way to nourish our friendship. Mid-year, we found ourselves in the midst of a global pandemic. To accommodate the virus, we created a COVID-19 poem form: 19 syllables and — as a nod to social-distancing — double-spaced lines.

We selected some of our favorite poems and put them in this book. We hope you enjoy reading them. We certainly enjoyed writing them.

Gail
Ann
Kate

Nonet	Lune 2	Didactic Cinquain
Butterfly Cinquain	Haiku Sonnet	Tanka
Imayo	Dodoitsu	Hay(na)ku
Shadorma	Arkquain	COVID-19
Lune 1	Cinquain	

Nonet

9 lines
syllables descending:
9 - 8 - 7 - 6 - 5 - 4 - 3 - 2 - 1

before the freeze, three days of sun, warmth
see the people mowing their lawns
cleaning and fixing windows
caulking cracks big and small
stop for a minute
and give deep thanks
there's a place
you call
home   AR

we want to hold onto memories
fearing impairment of the mind
but that which we remember
so often causes pain
could we be relieved
just a little
grief might be
more tame
then   GH

each morning there are big decisions
do I send this poem or that one?
is this the place for the truth,
emotional haiku?
or practice restraint
and write about
this cat here
alert
still   AR

reporting my life to a journal
is an act of faith in itself
the criteria are these:
pages just the right size
friendly pen and ink
supportive chair
leafy view
willing
heart   KT

don't mean to pry, just a suggestion
prepare a room in your deep soul
two chairs facing each other
now grief can come and sit
and you can have some
conversations
for the rest
of your
life   AR

there should be a good word to describe
the type of depression, malaise,
the troubling anxiety,
nauseating outrage,
the level of shock
the deep heartache
that is now
the norm
lies   GH

when everything is said and done
will we still tell ourselves nonsense
about how good things happen
to people who've been good,
how illness results
from bad choices
it's so hard
to face
truth   GH

our president, the "stable genius"
declaring that we must protect
our geniuses: Elon Musk,
and Thomas Edison;
and our inventions
the lightbulb and ...
the wheel. yes ...
the wheel
oy   AR

a circle of good Quaker women
listening as one of them mourns
a lost job, a cancer year
something in the air says
this is important
sitting here now
so simply
nothing
more   KT

no northern lights but plenty of stars
the ones hidden by city's glare
visible here, free to shine
wonder filling the heart
the stars, the large lake,
good reminder
that we are
just so
small   AR

a towering sculpture of blankets
beaded ev'rything — hats, coats, jars
geometric pottery
Native American
generational
transmission to
girls, women
create
art   GH

no wonder I walk around confused
I am afflicted with too much
awareness, observation
for my own good and for
the good of others
I need to use
denial
it would
help   GH

anxiety appears in my hip
is it a tumor? no, not that
perhaps it's just an old joint
but then there's the headache
that ache in my eye
glaucoma? no
it's that I'm
leaving
home   GH

walking into the chemo treatment
he said "sorry I'm out of sorts"
"out of sorts," said I, "that's sad
we will get you more sorts"
"do they have them here?"
"I sure hope so"
"great" and then
we both
laughed   AR

dream I'm in a car, my tooth falls out
so I have to call my dentist
but dang! I can't find my phone
and while I search, a creep
grabs at my car door
so the only
way out was
to wake
up   KT

if I imagine I'm dreaming now
that I walk in a daylight dream
how will that change my seeing?
will I move with more care
curiosity
even wonder?
I wonder
so here
goes   KT

I'm getting used to limitations
and I mean boundaries and walls
as well as necessary
manners, restraint, mores
for what else is there
but acceptance
tactfully
trusting
life   GH

this is a part of life, isn't it?
blizzards, hard rain, dense fog; it sucks
good thing the heart can travel
the heart can find the beach
a quiet forest
a small chapel;
renewal,
finding
rest   AR

there's one thousand cookies on a plate
nine hundred and ninety-nine are
taken by a billionaire
who gives you the last one
saying: *be careful*
that immigrant
will take your
cookie
what??   AR

wow

to make a big shift, must I travel
to a land across the ocean?
I hope not because it's hard
to pack and plan and leave
the people, cats, house
I love so much
returning
is so
sweet   GH

while on the train I am reminded
of what is and then what is not
of being here and not there
when I'm in my safe house
the limitations
are equalled by
the bounty
that is
home   GH

at Logan Airport I got into
a Honda Fit with just my bag
my iPhone GPS, my
blind courage and hurtled
through Boston rush hour
traffic and lived
to tell you
about
it   KT

in the stabbing wind and swirling snow
this old shivering oak still stands
its crisp brown leaves flicking flakes
back into the pale air
it has earned its place
and trusts its roots
and knows its
native
ground   KT

how long has it been since I've seen you?
seasons get shorter and shorter
let us talk about our lives
and not skip over the
rich compost of grief
beauty will bloom
connection
laughter,
love   AR

9

authentic gratitude at the Fair:
reasonable humidity
bright blue sky, beautiful breeze
no fried food on a stick
just First Kiss apples,
Asian chicken
and water
so cold
wet   GH

life is like a complex labyrinth
no, it's like a jigsaw puzzle
with a few missing pieces
or maybe a racetrack.
I think I have it:
life is like air
or water
crucial
gift   GH

moon appears above the gazebo
a magical soft light; round, full
next morning, a diff'rent place
it moves as it changes
now only half-lit
it shows itself
shares the sky
with the
sun   AR

I read in the paper this morning
that no matter how much we're loved
no matter the number of
friends, lovers, colleagues, pets
or the jobs we've held
or what we've done,
we all die
alone
seul   GH

lush lucky lazy Minnesota
wrens and robins taking their ease
September squirrels unhurried
as they heft their acorns
from this yard to that   ·‿·
as if to say
relax there's
enough
time   KT

listening to the storyteller
watching the audience sigh, laugh;
rapt, they seem to all lean in
the art of the telling
what is the secret?
story's true heart
is how to
open
doors   AR

comparison is a big black hole
opening the door to sadness
dark voices on the shoulder
no matter what is done
it is not enough
so difficult
to stop this
sucking
sound   AR

last year it was recommended that
one baby aspirin is good
and now they tell us: no, no
do not take this daily
it will do you harm
so no wonder
neurosis
stakes its
claim   GH

does *absence make the heart grow fonder*
I am not sure I believe it
because this is also true:
out of sight, out of mind
it can't be both things
cast your ballot
primary
Tuesday
vote   GH

slowly the body will remember
how to wake in a heated house
will forget about sandals
and opening the door   ˙ ˙
wide to the morning   ‿
will forget screens
and how green
life can
be   KT

sunrise, humid like mid-summer time
mid-morning brings plain ol' summer
followed by late afternoon
perhaps a spring shower
then autumnal wind
Minnesota:
most seasons
in one
day   AR

storms and fires all over the world
while people are being murdered
why should I read the paper?
why should I end my day
aware of all this?
instead I gaze
at the moon
and feel
peace   GH

13

at the beginning of the massage
my mind is bouncing all around
like a puppy wild for play
strangely, within an hour,
the pup is face down
still as granite
don't make this
dead dog
rise   KT

the Earth is either a burning bush
or, in some places, Noah's Ark
this, the gift we've been given
it is worth fighting for,
it's worth becoming
a radical
this Eden
humans
trashed   AR

pathways, freeways, roads, narrow and wide
some so straight go on forever
others follow a river
twisting, no route to cross
all of these choices
we can only
take them one
at a
time   AR

just one of the people in the room,
I, like others perhaps, have thoughts
and feelings that are complex
so I don't expose them
too vulnerable
it would not do
any good
restraint
rules   GH

in Greek and Roman mythology
the food the gods ate had a name —
ambrosia — and immortals
were the only beings
allowed to partake
these tomatoes
now let us
break that
rule   KT

full plane, many seats, three on each side
with each seat, there's a monitor
with each monitor, choices
a choice to pass the time
or perhaps to sleep
entertain us
we cannot
simply
be   AR

if I wrote you a lengthy letter
words on paper, not computer
your name on the envelope
right hand corner, a stamp;
I can imagine
the joy you'd feel
opening
reading
love   AR

the world seems as though it's different
was there always this much bad news?
were there these kinds of crises
terrible leadership
when I was younger?
youth protects us
I suppose
lucky
kids   GH

after losing my favorite hat
I retrace all my steps, make calls
search the car, chastise myself
easy come, easy go
Grandad used to say
and so I leave
a trail of
winter
gear   KT

how I wish I understood cat speech
he makes so many diff'rent sounds
how do I know if he is
talking to himself or
saying something of
great importance?
what say you
vocal
cat?   AR

at the beginning of ev'ry day
I enter the morning hopeful
grateful for time and quiet
morning is the high point
the rest of the day
a steady rush
to live life
go out
tasks   GH

Now I wonder, have we always been
a callous violent people?
it's no good fooling ourselves
we arrived on these shores
torn traumatized and
hungry for a
chance to be
the top
dog   KT

17

loss is diff'rent when it is your own
grief is more than a visitor
a part of the garden now
swaying alongside love,
disappointment, hope;
flowers, not weeds,
all of them
part of
you   AR

to survive, we often tell ourselves
all kinds of things that are not true
like *I am doing my best,*
I chose the right person,
don't know how I feel,
if I defer
I'll be loved,
I'm nice:
lies   GH

many events happened on this day
politics, conundrums, grief, hope
in the midst of all of this
you arrive in the world
and all of us are
better for it
happiest
birthday
you   AR

flip the switch to turn on the furnace
and you've set winter in motion
no way you can stop it now
go ahead, roast turkeys
deck the goddam halls   ·ᵕ
with never-greens
sing till you
forget
June   KT

an old dog wearing a gray jacket
he's tethered to a purple leash
it's held by black mittened hands
the human's heavy coat
a dark shade of green
this cold morning
as always
linked in
love   AR

I must look like a comedy act
trying to water hanging plants
with my new telescoping
hose attachment as though
I know what to do
only I fail
no washer
it soaks
me   GH

19

various shades of green now displayed
tulips, little dots of color
people plant pots of pansies
it was winter here once
monochromatic
the Earth has its
seasons and
so do
we   AR

I miss the amniotic delight
of sinking into a hot bath
but a sauna is next best
lying on smooth cedar
feet up mind adrift
sweating till I'm
submerged in
my own
sea   KT

reflecting on the time remaining
(not that we ever know how long)
finite possibilities
infinite desires
have to make choices
get serious
go forward
before
death   GH

all along I've been aware of death
as a comrade who walks with me
and tells me these worries I
swat like gnats are normal
you will discover
it's all okay
dear, she says,
I've got
this   KT

Butterfly Cinquain

9 lines

syllables:

2 - 4 - 6 - 8 - 2 - 8 - 6 - 4 - 2

inside
these bare branches
are small preparations
for what I barely imagine
green buds
in the womb now beneath the bark
needing just sun and time
someday my eyes
will see   KT

adverbs
consistently
describe any old verb,
and their first cousins, adjectives
exist
to enhance and to modify
nouns: people, places, things
my sweet cat sleeps
soundly   GH

walking
as minutes pass
sounds, smells intensify
these people, where did they come from?
they stroll
some roll along in their wheelchairs
at nine-thirty, clutching
cookie buckets
the Fair   AR

coffee
its importance
is so ridiculous
constant search for the perfect cup
give up
remember what is critical
and what is good enough
it's not coffee
it's love   GH

her dog
Sadie sat still
with effort, one ear cocked,
shining eyes trained on the server
who held
the plate of hot pesto pasta
high and so hopelessly
out of any
pet's reach   KT

I had
only three aunts:
Mary, Zillah and Ruth
my little family dwindles
with time
now Ruth is the last one to leave
it seems appropriate
she loved a good
party   AR

sitting
in doc's office
wearing sad little gown
how many times will I do this
I mean
so far I can still go to her
but I know that someday
she'll have to come
to me   KT

the words
should, must, ought, do
are words of my father
they could be from a policeman
the words
later, not now, after a while
belong to my mother
who was busy
reading   GH

slogans
they will get old
tiresome like jingles
twenty twenty, hard to resist
a chant
for this critical election
twenty-twenty vision
needed, of course,
to vote   GH

birthdays
can be quicksand
they can be helium
a quiet place for reflection
perhaps
or an opportunity to
look at the compass and
then say out loud:
onward!   AR

amen
to discipline
for its own humble sake
to show up, sit on the cushion
say yes
count the breaths or the syllables
trust that this universe
has nourishment
enough   KT

open
I think that's it
an invitation to
reveal in kind and to expose
oneself
which is what intimacy is
so go ahead and try
be authentic
real   GH

yearning
for endless walks
on rocky desert trails
smelling mesquite and juniper
and sun
marveling at striated cliffs
carrying just water,
a stick, a song
no more   KT

this life
made up of small
moments strung together
there is so much yet to be done,
savored
humans, do you think we can learn,
reject evil, embrace
the beauty of
the world?   AR

lilacs
lavender blooms
under a deep, gray sky
are they emitting their own light?
rain falls
this is also a part of spring
the unpredictable
sudden growth is
magic   AR

grammar
punctuation
the beauty of commas
periods and semi-colons
helpers
they keep words and thoughts organized
writing's infrastructure
like traffic lights
saves lives   GH

the cry
from my oak tree
so poignant and so dire
ev'ry three seconds a young bird
hungry
or lonely calls for company
or aid or some small sign
that this summer
won't end   KT

mother
everyone
has one, even orphans
we all exit our mother's womb
and then
the rest is chance or luck or fate
invisible mother
always with us
till death   GH

my cat
his inner life
(I believe he has one)
he studies, watches me open
the door
if he is not thinking things through
why does he deliver
his best toys to
my shoe?   AR

waiting
to be blessed by
the colors of springtime
greens pinks lavenders and yellows
my heart
stirring at the thought of lilacs
bowing to these dreams of
crocus primrose
tulip   KT

Friday
relief today
almost done with the week
still standing, observing beauty
also
all the hardships, difficulties
worries about the world
yet we made it
Friday   GH

this day
smell, sight, touch, sound
gardens prepare to rest
get out the flannel, hints the breeze
seasons
can only be experienced
beautiful, sensual,
experience
autumn   AR

mornings
feel so precious
pristine, another chance
to wake and see this universe
anew
in gardens of the possible
freshly, briefly, dew shines
morning glories
open   KT

sinus
odd cavity
acoustical drum-like
also the breeding ground for germs
gross thought
little hollow spaces of glop
getting so infected
to the rescue:
Z-pak!   GH

walking
with awareness
we are all from somewhere
our bodies and our DNA;
landscape
brings my ancestors here today
in snow and ten degrees
they'd nod and say
chilly   AR

worry
anxiety
they are both living here
sitting at the big round table
good news
other residents: contentment
joy, creativity,
wonder give it
balance   AR

today
the gentle sky
is filled with spring perfume
throngs of infant leaves bow and sway
bluebells
nod as if to say *go ahead,*
take a chance, put away
those warm gloves and
wool hats   KT

firstborn
a position
you are just born into
you had no say in the matter   ·:)
relax
it's not your fault you took the brunt
of what they did not know
at each stage of
childhood   GH

big cat
I remember
when you were two months old
curious, out in a new world
and now
outside sounds startle; you are brave
and have learned a few things
happy you play
with me   AR

Rilke
what a poet
maybe my favorite
let ev'rything happen to you ...   ·:)
there's more!
solitude is everything ...
no feeling is final ...
just keep going ...
wisdom   GH

online
I'm searching for
a new warm friendly hat
there seems to be one in Finland
how sad
to imagine the lovely Finn
knitting and mailing it
when I know I'll
lose it   KT

fat flakes
snow falls quickly
a footprint turns to ice
as the temp'rature takes a dive
freezing
sun growing stronger, looks around
what the hell happened here?
ice, snow ... I will
melt you   AR

time warp
Thursday vanished
waking up each morning
like Ground Hog's Day repetition
it seems
(as I wake in my bed at dawn)
each day lies ahead like
a long highway
out West   GH

nothing
is a strange word
after you utter it
the metamorphosis begins:
nothing —
a pronoun, adjective, adverb
made of seven letters
can't hide that it's
something   GH

photos
celebrations
from all around the world
the calendar turns east to west
we vow
to take better care of ourselves
resolutions are made
perfect time to
begin   AR

inside
this package of
imported organic
Turkish figs I find one black hair
which serves
as a kind of secret signal
from the tired harvesters
remember us
we're real   KT

travel
leave here, go there
and then there's the return
we repeat this to get away
from here
because we need new perspectives
because we feel burned out
from our own lives
stop, pause   GH

voices
live in my head
some guide while others block
I made room for them in childhood
but now
creativity demands this:
all of you get out, please
and let me do
my Work   AR

this man
burns like a sun
his anger is righteous
his words pour from a molten heart
his blaze
is unlike the destroying fires
set by the other ones
the ones who love
to hate   KT

driving
on dry pavement
with small, icy patches
a landscape rolls in brown and white
wind blows
a bird flies by so close to me
so bright around it's neck
a red ring — *fly*
pheasant   AR

house guests
winter doldrums
arrive with suitcases   ‥⌣
I ask them *how long will you stay?*
they say
we like you, so we'll stay a while
I say *no guest room here*
They say *no need*
I sigh   GH

secret
don't tell the kids:
birthdays change as you age
no Pin the Tail on the Donkey
no cake
just mounds of awe and gratitude
for verticality
being alive
enough   GH

morning
I walk in it
attempting to stay clear
except my mind loves a chew toy
drop it!
let thoughts flow freely in and out
better yet, let's focus
do our best not
to trip   AR

objects
live and breathe too
in ev'ry room they wait
listening and watching for our
return
their expectant voices humming
their trillions of atoms
twirling tiny
batons   KT

time flies
some people say
I think I disagree:
time moves slowly, predictably
it walks
or strolls or ambles, never flies
it sometimes seems to sit
lollygagging
derailed   GH

they say
that a bad start
predicts a good journey
that can apply to a whole life
perhaps
it matters where we hope to go
how much we can carry
how gracefully
let go   KT

bungee
you get strapped in
for the trip of your life
elaborate mechanism
insane
what people won't do for some thrills
gravity defying
thrown toward heaven
death wish   GH

summer
will not give up
it's enthusiasm
will not be lessened even when
light fades
the tomatoes are ripening!
the fair has not begun
summer will not
relent   AR

Lily
in her gap year
learns by trial and error
the ancient art of bookmaking
slowly
with paper string needle scissors
a sense of adventure
copious glue
and hope   KT

these birds
do not worry
they awaken each day
knowing what they must do: survive
aware,
keep the nest safe, find food, water
stressful, sure — but best not
to have many
choices   AR

they fight
about who's right
it's not what it's about
I remind myself quietly
listen
let the theme show up like magic
from under the black hat
a white rabbit
appears   GH

praise for
autumn's spirit
its generosity
the brave bountiful sacrifice
of leaves
teaching us about letting go
and showing us also
how falling is
freedom   KT

morning's
hygiene routine
meanwhile the market tanks
institutions have been sloppy
again
greed rules, bureaucracy falters
yet somehow one by one
we cope, we keep
going   KT

some days
I doubt myself
cannot find my way out
(okay, it's most days, let's be real)
but look,
a beautiful, clear day arrives
suddenly all things are
possible, I
say: *yes*   AR

Imayo

4 lines
syllables: 7 — 5 each line

zinnias are Mexican — daisies speak français
cosmos come from Paraguay — snapdragons from Spain
Canadian coneflowers — Japanese dogwood
my own United Nations — beauty ev'rywhere

GH

if I could bottle these days — summer perfection
I would uncork them in March — maybe the 15th
suddenly the gray would melt — no slush, no slogging
no wish to get on a plane — paradise right here

KT

reflections on the water — trestle bridge, trees, sky
crew teams glide four to a scull — ripple the vision
they are moving quietly — dividing a cloud
dark waters close behind them — restore the picture

AR

anxiety at my door — I welcome it in
it stomps around in big boots — I sit, ignore it
perhaps you would like some tea? — I gently offer
anxiety growls, sits down — conversation starts

AR

I keep on asking myself — not a real question
more like an exclamation — a plea into air:
how did we elect this man — a sociopath
we all knew how it would go — the toll it would take

GH

ev'rything is connected — ankle to the shin
ovary to uterus — stamen to pistil
even parts of speech connect — adverbs with their verbs
and yet on dark, lonely nights — I feel all alone

GH

centennial of suffrage — and who do we have?
rich, white men making the rules — how will we change this?
voting may not be enough — rotten with money
civil disobedience — we still have a voice

AR

a cow standing in a field — a key in a door
a girl in a party dress — a valentine card
a train leaving the station — three coins in a bowl
from what universe of dreams — do these things arise?

KT

a big taste of Trinidad — curried lamb, rice, dal
how to live, lead a just life — our conversation
if all the world could join us — we are fortunate
come together, share the food — neighbors together

AR

overnight, dusted with snow — all rooftops now white
lines run house to pole to house — cable, electric
there are five lines, four spaces — a musical staff
birds as notes, chickadee lands — that would be an "A"

AR

I remember ev'ryday — how lucky I am
to be alive and doing — moving and thinking
to have a good friend, a cat — the greatest pleasures
to have faced the biggest fear — and to have survived

GH

what's that unusual sound — my hearing, still good
oh, where is it coming from — I'm tracking it down
rhythmic, with a little squeak — from the dining room
when I locate it, I sigh — young Momo, snoring

AR

driving north, trees almost bare — lakes overflow banks
acres once rolling with green — the sun turns them gold
she says *who would live out here? — middle of nowhere*
I keep my thoughts to myself — it looks like heaven

AR

the small pump inside my chest — wants my attention
it's telling me with each beat — give up divisions
let go of too much thinking — abstain from whining
be in love with your people — live whole-heartedly

KT

learning only ends at death — as far as we know
of course we could be so wrong — when life is over
education might begin — not so full of facts
creative curriculum — after we're done here

GH

what if Christmas was in June — leaving December
to be what it is, quiet — a time to be home
a calm transitional month — gateway to winter
as it is now, we can't wait — for it to be done

GH

give a child eight pots of paint — here's what will happen
she'll mix them on the paper — till there's only mud
give her just three bright colors — red, yellow, and blue
then watch as she creates works — of wild vivid truth

KT

woman sleeps fully reclined — her husband nearby
some of the songs, her feet move — while the others sing
he whispers in Norwegian — blue eyes flutter, shine
fed and cared for, they are here — not what they wanted

AR

I always ask this question — I know it's crazy
is there something wrong with me? — I told you it's nuts
but you see, I never fit — never felt normal
and now I'm 71 — I don't care as much

GH

trying the B-flat once more — pressing till it burns
why is it so difficult — to get a clear tone
it's a simple instrument — just four nylon strings
my index finger whimpers — *I need a callus*

KT

we have cataracts removed — and shoulders mended
hips and knees and teeth replaced — still we persevere
wearing out gradually — like the couch cushion
I keep turning and fluffing — fluffing and turning

KT

the opposite of insight — stubborn compartments
refusal to see clearly — a false protection
we weave elaborate webs — stories we believe
so many ways to feel safe — hiding seems to work

GH

what happens in a greenhouse — humidity forms
the respiration of plants — water on the glass
outside the sun is shining — sky cloudless, pure blue
here inside it is raining — a gentle weeping

AR

last darkest day of the year — good time to gather
each person is their own gift — in a unique way
tonight, ev'rything slows down — there is renewal
it is a long year ahead — we carry the light

AR

with its one brown trembling leaf — this tree is waiting
having made it through winter — now it holds its breath
feeling for what will come next — wind, snow or torrents
good tree, we admire your poise — we hold on like leaves

KT

like the weather or your luck — friendships ebb and flow
some get buried, some exhumed — others carry on
can't be sure of anything — nothing stays the same
better rely on yourself — standard wise advice

GH

it is not what it's about — never ever is
all of this is metaphor — I hate to leave home
it is not about the house — but rather change, loss
putting things in a suitcase — could be a coffin

GH

winter storms will plague the East — Midwest waves goodbye
the sun makes an appearance — a warm assistant
we enter winter's cycle — melting and freezing
hope for more snow and less ice — and walk carefully

AR

being a Minnesotan — means knowing these sounds
shovels scraping on sidewalks — car engines groaning
thick boots stomping on doormats — cold hinges squealing
voices muffled by thick scarves — furnace kicking on
                                                        KT

thinking of what's important — cats, flowers, writing
this is personal, of course — to you, it might be
something very different — like God, exercise
opera, travel or dance — just know what you need
                                                        GH

when the moonlight woke me up — I looked out and saw
my oldest trustworthy friend — the moon, round and full
she has been my protector — reliable love
even when obscured by clouds — I know she is there
                                                        GH

take apart the fountain pen — cover, barrel, nib
run water through, it flows black — becoming clearer
clean pieces sit on the cloth — end of maintenance
I know there are other pens — they do not have soul
                                                        AR

my brain was in slow-motion — a sleepy weekend
or is this part of aging — the body reacts
back hurts, hands ache, neck is sore — how did this happen
I did not see this coming — youth ebbing this way

GH

man boarding the crowded bus — bandaged and limping
wide smile shows his missing teeth — his clouded eyes shine
I'm half-black, half-blind, he says — *and I'm beautiful*
we squeeze to make room for him — our angel stranger

KT

old couple lived in the house — I think they both died
new couple tears down the house — takes trees, French lilacs
they'll build themselves a palace — complete with a pool
just who do they think they are? — King Tut's relatives?

GH

my new car's slightly nervous — it's her first winter
tires defrosters bun-warmers — all ready to go
at icy intersections — she shrieks *Yikes! What's this?*
I say *It's Minnesota — you'll get used to it*

KT

a hawk in the neighborhood — it is not welcomed
crow, in pursuit, caws madly — what is it saying?
hawk! get away from our nests — away from our food!
two crows, now they are a team — the hawk flies away

AR

if I'd started these poems — around age fifty
my math says I'd have, by now — more than eight-thousand
this fact helps me comprehend — geology's truth
how all those drops of water — can carve a canyon

KT

curiosity kills cats — this is a saying
well, I think it could kill me — if I'm not careful
maybe this means I'm a cat — disguised as a girl
I nap, I like cleanliness — I've been known to purr

GH

when pen is put to paper — poem, lyric, song
creativity engaged — painting, cooking, craft
deep loneliness fades away — doesn't disappear
finds a chair, comfortable — and sits quietly

AR

the only things that bring calm — in times of deep grief
are gratitude and nature — so I say thank you
for being able to think — to walk and feel love
as I stroll under the stars — or look up at trees

GH

the black-brown bark-covered limbs — reach past my
    window
they are gnarled and mighty arms — offering bounty
sheaves of leaves green, then orange — now copper or
    bronze
teaching alchemy, saying — *learn how to do this*

KT

in a house across the street — there is suffering
desperation and sadness — oozing from the walls
perhaps this is happening — in more than one house
maybe in all our houses — would we admit it?

GH

the land rolls and then flattens — soybeans and then corn
fields and fields of sunflowers — all facing the sun
old tree stands solitary — with no companions
and if there's a storm coming — tree will see it first

AR

October's a tricky month — of fickle weather
scheming Columbus arrives — in his greedy ship
Spiderman masks, witch faces — stare from Walgreen's
    shelves
ev'rywhere avalanches — of sad candy corn

KT

capable of selfishness — generosity
mean, thoughtless, and destructive — full of love, kindness
tearing things and people down — building, nurturing
species is evil and good — and so confusing

AR

Shadorma

6 lines
syllables:
3 - 5 - 3 - 3 - 7 - 5

eagles soar
migration happens
birth happens
death happens
and none of this is novel
stars twinkle at night

GH

who would guess
an open window
sash lifted
breeze wafting
could be so mesmerizing
inspiring wonder

KT

fewer friends
more acquaintances
choosing to
separate
the wheat from the chaff, embrace
authenticity

AR

stood and watched
a grinning squirrel
dash across
the school lawn
two great green walnuts captured
one in each fat cheek

KT

in April
spring starts to move in
boxes of
daffodils
but winter is a squatter
refusing to leave

AR

two cats here
Olive and Momo
they love treats
warmth, cat food
how is it I'm so lucky:
feline Godmother

GH

tenacious
I identify
with winter
I'm stubborn
I don't back off easily
leaving is painful

GH

nursing home
we begin to play
her arms lift
gracefully,
from her wheelchair she conducts
delight on her face

AR

tomatoes
August's gift to us
let's cook them
eat them raw
let their juiciness fill us
till this time next year

GH

Best Western
breakfast room buffet
couple reads
sports section
soccer teammates with bed hair
attack their waffles

                    KT

now we meet
Jesus Christ lizard
there he is
observing
when he comes down from the tree
he walks on water

                    AR

religion:
people wandering
unaware
the answer
inside each one; still they ask
where is the Savior?

                    AR

frost warning
it's May's reminder
we live here
in the North
nature's working to uphold
our reputation

GH

lilac buds
stay curled in themselves
having heard
predictions
one more snow then you can burst
and perfume the sky

KT

when people
go on vacations
what are they
vacating
maybe they merely need a
diff'rent perspective

GH

bike travel
on cold winter streets
snowy schmutz
I travel
simultaneously strong
and vulnerable

AR

younger trees
flexibility
in their limbs
older ones
their roots deep, their trunks solid
with branches, swaying

AR

gratitude
critical at times
remember
who you love
what brings you joy and meaning
your luck and your mind

GH

catching up
the day slipped away
it started
in my car
my routine, interrupted
as I left the house

GH

celebrate
in this special room
protected
dark forces
cannot enter here — they do
not have a ticket

AR

hard to tell
where a breath comes from
from the air
or the gut
or the ground under my feet
hungrily rising

KT

old saying:
prepare for the worst
hope for the
best; good for
any, all situations
we may be facing

AR

no wonder
cynicism rules
it makes sense
in these times
what else can we do to cope
but use dark humor?

GH

containers
we call them bodies
ev'rything
is held there
organs, blood, bones, memories
like urns, they're sacred

GH

cloud shadows
on the Atlantic
illusion
created
dark shapes, looking so solid
from high up, islands

AR

snowflakes dance
on April's green buds
they are ghosts
of August's
bees and gnats come back to haunt
and to remember

KT

morning light
filters through the leaves
neighborhood
set design
or are we living inside
a watercolor

AR

it's arrived
overnight, it seems
wake to rain
autumn gray
damp chill direct to the bones
the season of tea

AR

responding
I made a career
responding
listening
to the dreams and the stories
all the unmet needs

GH

to questions
involving planning
I need time
like the dog
who turns circles on her bed
before she settles

KT

sweet to hear
neighbors talk and laugh
in this small
coffee shop
a nation undivided
ma's and pa's and kids

KT

who I love
becomes crystal clear
as I leave
this city
with suitcase in hand, I know
they will be with me

GH

no feelings
no experience
with Easter
eggs, bunnies
I never understood why
something about Spring

GH

Naomi
that lovely poet
once offered
a koan
ev'rything brings something else
I know what this means

KT

family
mine dwindles; am I
choosing mine?
or am I
forever on the outside
never belonging?

AR

take a walk
the birds are singing
dark, but yes,
spring will come
even in the worst of times
oh, the flowers bloom

AR

no one knows
that I wear his watch
and the time
ticks away
wrist to wrist, his and now mine
minutes, hours, years

GH

second place
will this always be
where women
stall, get stuck
in leading our sick country
won't this ever change?

GH

abusers
manipulators
skilled bullies
oh humans
a large, rough ocean demands
boatloads of courage

AR

on its shelf
the poinsettia
still lingers
crimson leaves
recalling the holidays
and waving goodbye

KT

making friends:
there is no pamphlet
explaining
the way to
reveal oneself honestly —
just give it your best

GH

this Sunday
is a holiday
easy to
celebrate
it's National Popcorn Day
what could be better?

AR

here it is
the eighteenth of March
a new day
one more chance
to live awake and aware
to bloom like flowers

KT

Lune 1

3 lines
syllables: 5 - 3 - 5

before breakfast time
I worry
about dinner plans

AR

home, my habitat
where I thrive
where I am rooted

GH

autumn is on pause
graciously
nodding to summer

GH

there's work and there's Work
it matters
one springs from the soul

AR

Midwestern morning
and here's this
Best Western breakfast

my nurse friend warns me
don't eat those
industrial eggs

KT

I thought I liked kids
but this one
tested that theory

GH

heirlooms and Sungolds
tomatoes
best part of August

GH

birds reporting in
as dusk falls
summer's sweetest sound

KT

overgrown garden
perfect place
for cat explorer

AR

park under fall trees
and your car
is decorated

KT

people walking by
their heads down
a hawk unnoticed

AR

dark-as-night morning
soon will end
fake daylight savings

GH

longest day, who cares?
time is time
but oh my, the light

AR

nothing is easy
certainly
not love, not dying

GH

tattered by cat play
the red cube
always bounces back

shredded by long use
my worries
wobble yet they stand

KT

76

reincarnation
please let me
come back as a cat

GH

air, cool and humid
beautiful
respite from the heat

AR

Creeping Charlie grows
tenacious
small purple flowers

AR

expected outcome
always death
why are we surprised?

GH

may I remember
slow green days
full of dappled light

KT

the birds fin'lly come
the right mix
black oil, peanuts, seeds

GH

nation of millions
leaderless
primed for tragedy

KT

fog blurs the treetops
as lies blur
a nation's outline

KT

layers of snow melt
native grass
once buried, rises

AR

a virus finds me
the world is
a large petri dish

AR

I abandoned me
yes, I did
a form of self-harm

GH

in front of the light
each morning
battling darkness

AR

winter of sorting
no wonder
I dream of laundry

KT

working late at night
my pleasure
it's a form of love

GH

trees stand sep'rately
their language
is hidden from us

AR

full moon in Dublin
lighting streets
while musicians play

GH

in stillness I feel
blood flowing
and I hear it sing

KT

farewell farewell to
summer light
hello candle flame

KT

the twin dog walkers
together
each morning, eight dogs

GH

adventure couple
never rest
they go, we watch them

AR

reading before sleep
and I smell
dad's pipe tobacco

AR

Lune 2

3 lines
words: 3 - 5 - 3

Tibetan prayer flags
yellow, green, white, red, blue
earth and elements

AR

season of goodbyes
orange and green and gold
sweeter than lilacs

KT

bee balm fading
still of interest to bees
food for birds

AR

woodpeckers and finches
live in my maple tree
better than houseguests

GH

drops of water
suspended from a red branch
waiting to fall

AR

maple branches blaze
a long loving fabulous farewell
to their leaves

KT

realization at dinner:
I really love the life
I have created

GH

Black-Eyed Susans
take the stage in autumn
soul-soothing flowers

AR

I imagine that
the State Fair is getting
grungy and sticky

GH

ukulele jam session
a circle of serious seniors
strumming four strings

KT

making no decision
very well may be the
worst decision ever

AR

why are children
not taught about solitude, loss
as inevitable realities

GH

watching leaves turn
how they droop, go limp
before they flare

KT

I'll tell you
who's tragic: it's Mike Pence
robotic Boy Scout

GH

neighbor's lawn sign
words of peace, unity, justice
a dog pees

AR

will I ever
read these old *New Yorkers*?
give it up

KT

tall dying sunflowers
become a buffet for squirrels
and beautiful finches

AR

autumn invites us
to become aware, engaged, thoughtful
to slow down

AR

horrible painful casualty
extinction of the koala bears
world burning up

GH

I am glad
caffeine, they say, is good
for the liver

AR

building a wall
plows shove ridges of snow
they are Republicans

AR

searching for words
to describe our nation's year
violent unsettling bizarre

KT

glisten like diamonds
tiny droplets on thin branches
winter's own beauty

GH

I wake up
and say, *today is Sunday*
I didn't die

GH

a Midwest storm:
I'm in love with here
morning turns dark

GH

keeping me company
gift that lasts all week
the Sunday *Times*

GH

until the wealthy
have their eyes opened wide
nothing will change

AR

absence of yearning
I want to feel relieved
accept what is

GH

that last Lune
was about authenticity, in case
I was vague

GH

heart is set
on a peaceful, quiet day
heart so silly

AR

do not stand
in the way of ideas
let them enter

GH

my therapist said
solitude is different from isolation
one feeds you

AR

too much green
tends to block the view
I welcome autumn

KT

many resort people
are they all successful in
leaving worry behind?

AR

Haiku Sonnet

Four 3-line haiku
5 - 7 - 5 syllables per haiku
plus a final couplet of either
5 or 7 syllables per line

on a child's seesaw
when is the exact moment
when up becomes down?

and with emotions
precisely when does normal
become disordered?

in friendships and love
can shifts in connection be
pinpointed in time?

and in bed, at night
is there a clear-cut second
between wake and sleep?

a person could go crazy
looking for these turning points

GH

a goldfinch, eating
sitting on a sunflower
in the cool, dry breeze

from the gazebo
my gray cat watches this feast
flower, bird, swaying

and does the goldfinch
know how beautiful he is,
yellow with black mask?

and does my cat know
his pursuit of the goldfinch
is just fantasy?

bright feathers flutter
the dream flies away

AR

falling out of love
not a popular subject
horribly painful

so few songs written
other than country-western
about this subject

but let me tell you
when projections fall away
what remains is true

a disappointment
(the dark side of projection)
stings as it suggests:

let go of your wishful dreams
grieve, and then get on with life

GH

in early morning
raindrops hang on window's edge
from night's stealth shower

wrens are whispering
about something someone sang
around three a.m.

far up a jet plane
finds a path over the clouds
trusting its radar

here, I awaken,
having trekked and voyaged with
multitudes, now dim

so much happens in the night
so many worlds pass through us

KT

peculiar time
it is not dependable
too much, too little

for students, it chugs
summer is too far away!
the clock ticks slowly

until one looks up
no longer at that small desk
how did I get here?

we assign it names:
second, minute, hour, week;
they are all moments

my mother, at ninety-two
sighs *it loses its meaning*

AR

lessons all day long
it is twenty-four seven
school is in session

self-care and kindness
gratitude one-oh-one, yes
that is a biggie

text books are varied
mine is not the same as yours
covers similar

slower than others
patience is necessary
life dyslexia

ev'ry morning the bell rings
university of life

AR

sometimes the signals
start to make a kind of sense
vague clues get clearer

it's a new message
a dog digging at the fence
trying to get through

or there's a midwife
at bedside reassuring
keep breathing, she says

it's hard to believe
something is coming to birth
in this discomfort

hard to imagine angels
standing waiting to applaud

KT

after autumn rain
sidewalk strewn with gold and brown
a scattered carpet

and the faint fragrance
of school days in Illinois
and the yellow bus

the rustle and scrape
of gym shoes kicking through leaves
the sweetest music

then downhill at dusk
and crossing the yard toward home
smelling fresh-baked bread

crust golden and center soft
as a child's dream of heaven

KT

the part of the world
that is visible to us
is not all there is

we see trees, streets, sky
but unless we're snorkeling,
in a submarine,

or scuba diving,
the undersea universe
is largely unseen

you think you know me
but you know only a part
just a small amount

deep feelings, invisible
kept safe, albeit submerged

GH

an important thought
I want to remember this
but it could vanish

a beautiful day
I hope it's seared in my brain
it will fade, I know

music so sublime
it transports me to heaven
sadly, not for long

connections, people
relationships that feel good
and I know they change

this is our life, I suppose
thriving, grieving, accepting

GH

today is the day
to cross the Mississippi
over a long bridge

on foot is the best
cross the first time looking north
cross again, gaze south

pause often, lean out
be overwhelmed by raptures
red orange gold green

exclaim or sing out
praise for the faithful waters
rolling, rolling on

the best theater in town
standing room only, and free

                                        KT

solstice gathering
each year we begin, singing
Carolyn's Party .

conversation pods:
renovation, vacation
catching up on life

to welcome the light
we gather but once a year
this, then, is our tribe

solstice gathering:
we have more wine at the end
than when we started

solstice gathering
it makes us lighter

AR

when we were twenty
we shared a room in London
here we are again

borrowing sweaters
taking turns in the shower
setting our alarms

spring of '68
BBC brought us bad news
King and Bobby K

Paris rioted
Beatles sang *Sergeant Pepper*
Twiggy bared her legs

lives were unfolding
here, there, ev'rywhere

KT

a leaf on the bridge
wind from passing cars — it flies
it will be a bird

the life of a leaf
from spring to autumn, in storms,
there until it's time

some are swept and burned
some end up in a large pile
dogs, children jump in

ready, it takes off
lifted then kissed by the sun
look! it spins and twirls

on its way to the river
this one has a final dance

AR

evaluations
ev'ry time you turn around
you're asked the same thing:

would you be willing
to take a moment — tell us
how you feel about

your purchase, your food,
your experience with us,
did we treat you well

we want your feedback
if you have a few minutes
to stay on the line

I tell the robotic voice:
do your best, then go away

GH

preparing to write
should not be mistaken for
writing, creating

tasks before writing
are perhaps necessary
but let's be careful

not to confuse it
with the real art of writing
words, music, stories

sometimes we just need
to put away the lists, books
sit down, let it out

we can spend our life prepping
to live instead of living

GH

seven golden beets
the last from my garden plot
simmer on the stove

a tin of dried sage
a jar of dried lavender
lounging on the shelf

remnants of summer
reminders of the long days
and the show-off sun

the days of short sleeves
and long easy ev'ning walks
it was not a dream

lavender's perfume
says it was real

KT

the people I've loved
(the ones who are still alive)
have begun to change

their bodies (like mine)
are beginning to ache more
and they are shrinking

we lose bone, I guess
as well as hearing, vigor
and the dreaded loss:

our minds, memories
our senses of direction,
cognition, int'rests

at diff'rent speeds, we're going
toward the finale, goodbye

GH

lately I wonder
where a democracy goes
when it leaves our land

does it slink away
to hide and heal and wait to
reinvent itself

or evaporate
like water from brine leaving
its savor behind

maybe it flees to
a fresh young nation or one
weary of tyrants

perhaps it returns to our
founders asleep in their graves

KT

individuals
sit in a semi-circle
walkers and wheelchairs

they smile, tap their feet
most of them can sing along
one woman, sleeping

a visitor sits
close to her sockless father
holds his hand and sings

my isolation
is nothing compared to theirs
and I can break mine

music surrounds them
they are less alone

AR

at Lake Harriet
watching the sun rise at 6
I concentrated

focused all my thoughts
on my mentor, a great man
who is in D.C.

in the hospital
waiting for his surgery
I became aware

this is what prayer is
sending love and strong wishes
through the air for miles

so that the surgeon would know
his patient is deeply loved

GH

holiday season
it's here again already
ask me if I care

carols cards shopping
my interest is zero
I'll just wait it out

even for Christians
who love the baby Jesus
isn't it tiring?

so predictable
shepherds and wise guys and a
Herod so like ours

Santa, all I want this year
is January second

KT

light dusting of snow
we are not done with this yet
wind blows cold, gusting

transitional time
days of sun are days of hope
birds become active

look at the garden
messy, sure, but underground
possibilities

we are all seeds now
pushing up through the darkness
in search of warmth, light

the garden stands alone as
the easiest metaphor

AR

feeling old today
I guess it will be like this
inevitable

our bodies break down
there's no question about that
but it seems crazy:

once you finally
acquire enough wisdom
to know who you are

you begin that slide
toward diminished energy
not enough time left

if you warn a young person
they will never believe you

GH

we were once too young
to know about one lone truth:
life begins, life ends

if one is lucky
suffering is minimal
but it still happens

cynicism comes
hand in hand with bitterness
a lovely couple

send them somewhere else
don't let them take their shoes off
they damage the heart

we've lived a life now
we know to choose love

AR

may I not, she said,
rush past my healers in my
fierce search for a cure

may I not offend
all the lovely lanterns by
favoring darkness

we will all die of
something but somehow so far
we are still alive

in Sonoran heat
doves are cooing in the shade
of palo verde

no song is in me today
only this endless singing

KT

practicing, writing
nagging to-dos left outside
intimate and known

creativity
solitary endeavor
not a team player

feeling of fullness
and simultaneously
of deep loneliness

anguish and relief
discontent, bliss, misery
a writer's known friends

each moment tells me
this is where you live

AR

my mind is fuzzy
the doctors said it would be
they gave good advice

be very careful
don't drink wine or drive a car
sip lots of water

I listen to them
I kiss the hems of their smocks
they are smart and kind

were the drugs stellar?
yes, I was high for awhile
I loved ev'ryone

we're grateful tonight
me and my colon

KT

too tired to bathe
I'll postpone till tomorrow
and start the day clean

I need to be sharp
as people start to file in
to tell me their tales

and I will want to
listen and be completely
focused on each one

I keep their stories
heartbreaks, secrets, confessions
in my head and heart

I will need to be alert
the morning shower will help

GH

man on the spectrum
a Sunday morning patient
(I love what I do)

I get to listen
and I mean really listen
all the stories, tales

the heartache, turmoil
truth is told, grieving begins,
conflicts get resolved

a couple sits down
needing to be understood
accepted, heard, seen

something that I was not taught:
therapists must be real

GH

now I remember
lying on the flowered couch
with the chicken pox

through the big window
watching the neighborhood kids
laughing, playing tag

the pang of longing
the glass I couldn't pass through
the endless waiting

maybe in those hours
I vowed to claim this one life
to heal and to live

maybe I've kept that promise
maybe there are miles to go

KT

a web stretches from
hanging branch to the tree trunk
ambitious spider

this web is quite high
humans will not disturb it
spider chose wisely

it is visible
because the sun shines on it
she is there, tending

if a thread weakens
she nimbly goes to repair
one leg tugs, testing

and now it is The Waiting
the vibration of her meal

AR

warm summer morning
crossing over the river
airing out the brain

thoughts flow in and out
like air passing through a screen
a meditation

but wait, there's a bug
it does not pass through the screen
its name is Worry

beautiful river
I will stop to notice you —
the wind reverses

I breathe in and out
the bug blows away

AR

when I'm far from home
there are things to remember
to think of at night

when I'm lying in
an Irish bed, rain outside
thinking about home

remember: your friends
and your sweet cat, your children
they won't forget you

your home is waiting
it won't be mad you left it
it will welcome you

to go far away and then
return home: a miracle

GH

okay, now I'm mad
teardowns all over the place
houses get shredded

who has the right to
obliterate history
disturb birds, nature

this morning they took
a 200-year-old tree
thriving, enormous

in its place will be
a swimming pool and terrace
they should be ashamed

or arrested for murder,
larceny and selfishness

GH

again and again
with the two hands of my mind
I feel for the place

I mean the portal
the fissure in the earth or
the cleft in the sky

through which the stories
slip from that world into this
confounding reason

sometimes we're lucky
we catch one as it escapes
from its hidden house

we don't know how we did it
and no witness was present

KT

yellow bicycle
we ride across town, traffic
does not bother us

some drivers are pissed
we don't really care, in fact,
it gives us pleasure

we are colorful
yellow bike, purple jacket
we are visible

ah, but be aware
of cars, glass, sand and potholes
many obstacles

how far have we gone?
how far will we go?

AR

many ways to lie
to not tell yourself the truth
sweet self-deception

the mechanisms
we all hear so much about
are both friends and foes:

one is projection
followed by sublimation
maybe regression

the most common one
(my personal favorite)
is ol' denial

we bury disappointment
beneath beautiful gardens

GH

will I have to leave
in order to remember
how much I love life

how grateful I am
for a home to take care of
for my bed, bathroom

for the trees outside
for my cat (my companion)
the people I love

will I have to leave
my ev'ryday life to see
all the beauty here

this is what I know: my love
is endless for this life here

GH

I remember this:
plates on tall sticks, all spinning
variety show

getting them started
not easy, but the trick is
to keep them whirling

one is slowing down
audience, almost as one
lets out a long *Oohhhhhhhhh!*

and what makes someone
develop a skill like this?
just something to do?

it isn't about the plates
truth is, it's all in the sticks

AR

131

thanksgiving each day
how 'bout we make that happen?
this week, it's commerce

table settings, cards,
books on how to be thankful;
you need to be taught?

your list must be long:
comfortable and well-fed
wanting for nothing

to be warm and safe
gratitude flows like honey
to love and be loved

now, go ahead. it's your turn
it won't cost you anything

AR

Dodoitsu

---

4 lines
syllables: 7 - 7 - 7 - 5

do you have a container
for storing anxiety?
I asked the store manager,
sadly he said, No

                    GH

lack of reciprocity
glaring brightly like neon
take stock, slow down, understand
people's diff'rences

                    GH

sun paints the eastern sky pink
leaves are slow to change color
still hanging onto their green
blue October sky

                    AR

so glad I'm not seventeen
when you don't know who you are
but you pretend that you do
not child, not adult

                    GH

when Mary Oliver wrote
joy's not made to be a crumb
did she mean it's the whole cake?
we should grab a fork

KT

December is a hard month
memories of vanished times
confusing paradoxes
old grief rises up

GH

how to wake knowing this day
could be my last yet live like
I've a hundred years to build
this work, stone by stone

KT

a piece of a song lingers
a loop, over and over
I cannot get rid of it
I curse the ear worm

AR

looking through these old journals
wondering which ones to toss
the oak outside my window
says *throw them, keep me*

KT

this world is full of spaces
buildings, open land, mind, heart
all with possibilities
to renew, create

AR

I can see what's in my way:
my very own neuroses
how much time have I wasted
ignoring my voice?

GH

my bamboo plant grows like corn
bright green and high and eager
soon the whole town will do this
it will seem normal

KT

you are born with it or not
it cannot be taught — maybe
copied, but then it's mimicked:
sensitivity

GH

outside my August window
an ancient oak branch swaying
I ask, *Is summer fading?*
and the whole branch nods

KT

bridges over the river
the water sparkles below
isolated in metal
one person per car

AR

four-thirty in the morning
a cool breeze through the window
walking across our bodies
thirteen pounds of cat

AR

we wait for *critical mass*
before passing strict gun laws
meanwhile we say mass for the
critically bled

KT

what I miss are school supplies:
new pencils with erasers,
pretty case to put them in,
some pens, paper, glue

GH

a cat discovers the world
with great curiosity
what is this? and now he knows
what a bee can do

AR

my day started with goslings
and then home to a surprise
people in the street, singing
Happy Birthday, love

GH

hair is like a Brillo pad
skin is moist and so sweaty
eyeglasses fog up outside
disgusting dew point

GH

fifty oak leaves on this branch
waving goodbye to summer
eight have already turned brown
overachievers

KT

man with a rake does his job
what washes up on the beach
what humans have discarded
he cleans up the mess

AR

a low rumble in the south
planes, sirens, and shifting clouds
even birds sound tentative
waiting for the storm

KT

a dose of reality
along with information
and courage to face fear, doubt:
that's security

GH

a short drive to Wisconsin
a trunk load of fireworks
but let's call them what they are:
explosives, small bombs

AR

car travel is a strange life
maps, coffee, trucks, gas stations
the steady search for restrooms
very little rest

KT

have you gone to bed and hoped
you would not see the next day?
the nurse asks at Urgent Care
and Happy New Year!

GH

I never learned to whistle
my upper lip has a scar
at four, I fell and it split
I remember blood

GH

four strings on my little uke
hard to remember their names
green cows eat arugula
G, C, E and A

KT

writing songs for many years
and all of them are bookmarks
reminders and reflections
where and who I was

AR

remove glittering snowflakes
from the sidewalks and driveways
the moon, waning, is still bright
floating in silence

AR

insurance card in my purse
shovel and boots in my car
phone charged and passwords hidden
safety is a myth

KT

people give advice about
how to pack and what to bring
they say: *just the essentials*
how can I pack love?

GH

I carry this photograph
the ship on Omaha Beach
what you went through, what happened
I will never know

AR

forget Buddhism, Scripture
forget the pithy sayings
instead, may I suggest we
read Mister Rogers

AR

I arrived home from the store
Olive, I said, *I bought you
a new flavor of cat food:
it's Rabbit Paté!*

GH

this weather is opera
the wind a mighty chorus
sunflowers sway, lift their heads
sing the aria

AR

buttered toast and fragrant tea
my morning thoughts reach out to
the hills and orchards and the
farmers of Hunan

KT

one of these years I'll go in
(my annual physical)
and there will be evidence
of tired organs

GH

rain swells, then decrescendos
leaves, light brushes on snare drums
over tympanic thunder
percussion concert

AR

what interests me is this:
people's true thoughts, unshared ones
kept hidden, little secrets
true fabric of self

GH

Arkquain

Three stanzas of 4 lines each
syllables:
1 - 2 - 3 - 4
5 - 7 - 7 - 5
4 - 3 - 2 - 1

The two 7-syllable lines must rhyme.
The first word of the first stanza
and the last word of the last stanza
must be the same.

here
the place
I always
and only am

not someplace future
not where I was yesterday
it's no simple thing to stay
where I am right now

a human thing
this challenge
to be
here   KT

gray
winter
my cat blinks
and settles in

post-Christmas dreaming
resting, popcorn in large bowls
take the time to set some goals
season internal

my cat is curled
a comma
warm and
gray   AR

space
a thing
that's no-thing
presence? absence?

it holds anything
it's older than history
let's call it a mystery
a wondrous koan

I could say more
if I had
enough
space   KT

back
the spine
vertebrae
we're vertical

which is the problem
surely the design should be
more similar to the knee
we are meant to crawl

a tall tower
of small bones
dicey
back   GH

park
crowded
crawling with
parents, children

taken for granted
beautiful, wide open space
now becomes their saving grace
a break from "normal"

now they stop, look
and ask: *where*
did we
park?   AR

flesh
so strange
and prone to
lumps viruses

bruises fevers sprains
now it seems most days I wake
expecting something to break
hoping for enough

resilience to
live in this
fragile
flesh   KT

luck
is like
anything
invisible

it's a noun, for sure
it's kind of like the word health
which is similar to wealth
words that are not things

untouchable
elusive
so good
luck   GH

film
over
a mirror
like damp cheesecloth

I peel it away
there stand all the souls I know
eyes serene and faces glow
my life's best teachers

gone but standing
more alive
than in
film   KT

chalk
adorns
the sidewalks
children artists

messages of hope
rainbows in bright blue, red, green
my young neighbor adds some scenes
my mind takes pictures

temporary
remember?
all is
chalk   AR

dreams
I wake
and forget
all that remains

a feeling a wisp
or this morning a man's name
Ponce de Leon whose fame
was that he searched for

fountains of youth
talk about
silly
dreams   KT

dark
absence
of sunlight
of perspective

when things are lit up
we feel safer, more in charge
all our problems not so large
which is more real?

life with lights on
or obscured
in the
dark?   GH

sleep
slumber
unconscious
essential time

the most important
time of the day is the night
critical we get it right
our brains need the rest

insomnia
a crisis
lack of
sleep   GH

fields
prairies
green and gold
I dream of this

long rural fencerows
and nothing to do but walk
and listen to grasses talk
as breezes move them

birds butterflies
all thriving
in my
fields   KT

lost
but here
a friendship
from long ago

memories return
now tapped, now released they flow
we were young, what did we know?
tilting at windmills

we discover
many ways
to be
lost   AR

154

spring
previews
coming soon
can't tell you when

sun higher, warmer
there is a scent in the air
and large sidewalk puddles where
once lay shining ice

oh my soul's soul
welcoming
seeds of
spring   AR

leap
into
this moment
it's all we have

so do not resist
the universe holds its breath
hoping we'll choose life not death
whatever that means

the soul will know
what's required
in this
leap   KT

mud
squishy
under all
this must be March

here we go again
longer days and shorter nights
grow some seedlings under lights
pump up the bike tires

ignore all those
Senators
slinging
mud   KT

breath
simple
yours and mine
air in air out

life is rare and brief
how many breaths will I get
I haven't used them all yet
may I greet each one

I've decided
that's my hope
with each
breath   KT

love
is like
the word *soul*
you can't see it

but it's essential
as is water, blood and air
when it's missing, you're aware
this is a crisis

panic sets in
transfusion
needed
love   GH

end
of life
issues, needs
are similar

to those of a child's
safety: do not fall or slip
well-being: state of kinship
a plan is needed

to advance toward
beginnings
or the
end   GH

frost
magic
beautiful
transformation

take this dull landscape
of bare trees and dirty snow
it's as if the season knows
how deprived we are

of breathtaking
wonder, art
made by
frost   AR

Cinquain

5 lines
syllables: 2 - 4 - 6 - 8 - 2

Gretchen
has a garden
like the one in Eden
all beauty and bounty except
no snakes

KT

pencils
of silver light
around my bedroom door
announcing to my dream-drenched eyes
the dawn

KT

my voice
my instrument
you are injured and bruised
tea for you and a good dose of
silence

AR

friendship
a form of love
not celebrated on
any holiday I know of
oh well

GH

dear Gail
you have tried hard
to understand, make sense
of all that has been gained and lost
now rest

GH

pretend
this is the end
how would you use today?
please answer this question and then
proceed

GH

tripping
on the cat toy
tripping on the cat toy
tripping on the cat toy — why not
move it?

AR

morning
favorite time
my cat has her routine
including being held by me
purring

GH

sun sends
a signal to
my sluggish winter feet
it's time to stop waiting and start
walking

KT

question
with no answer
so why bother asking
stop with the curiosity
shut up

GH

snowstorm
we flood the stores
stock up on essentials
as though we could really perish
winter

GH

grateful
to have a voice
I don't know how it works
but in times of heavy sorrow
I sing

AR

water
it's your season
appearing in all forms
rain, snow, ice; liquid then solid
I slip

AR

Didactic Cinquain

5 lines
Line 1: Noun
Line 2: Description of noun
Line 3: Action
Line 4: Feeling or effect
Line 5: Synonym of the initial noun

protest
fierce disagreement
sincere, brave, vulnerable
protecting our humanity
dissent

KT

books
human thoughts in print
revelations and imaginings
carrying me, speaking to me
volumes

KT

narcissism
a malady of our times
no empathy, constant need for attention
empty, stingy
self-absorption

GH

virus
well-being opposite
sneezing, head-pounding, coughing
leaving my body tired
sickness

AR

nap
a short period of sleep
daytime rejuvenation
rested, recharged
siesta

GH

laundry
sheets towels socks
it always comes around
life renewed again by simply
washing

KT

dreams
imagination, alive at night
unconscious activity
working life out
figments

GH

phone
connect, distract
switch-off, ignore, leave;
immediately feel adrift
cellular

AR

quiet
sound absence
chaos pushed aside
now there's room for contemplation
peace

AR

breath
bringer of life
enters, exits, enters, exits
mystery beyond knowing
inspiration

KT

sunshine
bright and blaring
spotlights every scene
beckons my soul to wake and see
radiance

KT

doldrums
sad day after day
surrounding you like fog
you tend to cry
gloom

GH

sleep
noun, verb
body, brain rests
restorative
slumber

AR

TV
shows us the world
news sitcoms commercials
everything but reality
the tube

KT

compass
directional guiding
showing true north
who you really are
guidance

AR

patterns
repetitive designs
arrangements within chaos
security
sequences

GH

defeat
absence of success
admitting failure
there is regret, shame
washout

GH

feet
body carriers
roaming, progress, ability
freedom
dactylus

AR

resilience
elastic survival
you keep getting up
determined
life force

GH

pretense
untrue presence
acting
fake and empty
dissembling

GH

breathing
in out in out
receiving oxygen
simple rhythm tells me I am
living

KT

bullies
intimidating, mean
inflict, damage, harm
making others feel small, powerless
oppressor

AR

garden
haven, blissful
growing, dirt-loving, blossoms
bringing hope
oasis

AR

quiet
absence of noise
still surroundings
peaceful, solace
serenity

GH

Tanka

5 lines
syllables: 5 - 7 - 5 - 7 - 7

leaning back watching
Tom Hanks as *Mister Rogers*
hearing muffled sobs —
the barely stifled weeping
of adults all around us

KT

letter carriers
have strange powers over me
each time I see them
out on the street my love flies
to them and sticks like a stamp

KT

an early morning
mid-October thunderstorm
rain: liquid, solid;
little white gumballs tossed down
bouncing on hard surfaces

AR

on my window sill
a fine avocado tree
leans into the sun
I grew it from a smooth seed
to prove that magic happens

KT

magical thinking
it's a good way to waste time
or maybe your life
it's reality that rules
not airy-fairy wishing

GH

grief's a visitor
without an invitation
and without warning
she is camouflaged by day
and at night, she comes alive

GH

maintaining balance
making more room for sorrow
taking in beauty
the outer world decaying
and the inner world blooming

AR

Whalan pastry shop
magnet for humanity
all bikers stop there
whatever their politics
it's One Nation Under Pie

KT

home sick, one hears sounds
diff'rent from the ones when well
viruses change brains
their voices are baritones
singing long dirges

GH

tallest sunflower
reaches up, seven feet high
I did not plant it
it fell from the bird feeder
one, tiny, powerful seed

AR

shadow on the wall:
a monster or a bad man
or a huge insect
it could be something pleasant
but it sure looks terrible

GH

lazy Saturday
little tasks slouch into line
to await their turn
chewing gum, looking around
hoping they won't be chosen

KT

anyone who thinks
cats are light with their small paws
has never heard, then,
my cat jump down, thud and grunt,
and walk across our bodies

AR

Momo performing
many cat yoga poses:
downward facing cat,
and, cleaning his butt, also
known as *Playing The Cello*

AR

in love with my cat
I'm not even embarrassed
she teaches me how
to love even when I'm scared
or when I'm preoccupied

GH

napping exploring
misplaced amorous attempts
brief bouts of wrestling
two cats can show us so much
about life in general

KT

overwhelmed people
how did we become this way?
is this inherent
in being alive, sentient
or is it American?

GH

lovely lovely snow
and me with no place to go
I could live like this
ears to hear and eyes to see
notebook, pen, and cup of tea

KT

I tell my own brain:
enough with the bizarre dreams!
don't remove Peter
but you can delete the rest:
the plane that falls and the shame

GH

there was a wedding
or perhaps a funeral
dreams seem to do this
conflate significant things
and invite us to wonder

GH

slip underwater
feel with your two hands to find
the sunken statue
of your forgotten knowledge
darker times need deeper skills

KT

others paint pictures
and you end up believing
it's what you look like
it's best not to allow them
to hang in your museum

AR

rare is the day when
the ground is reliable,
even, firm, no cracks;
and one walks with arms swinging,
easy, like clock pendulums

AR

driving home at night
after dinner with a friend
I say this out loud:
thank you for everything
bad days, losses, all of life

GH

baking's an art form
and a good use of winter
waking up early
to make a hearty cornbread
and the whole world smells like home

KT

November content
neither autumn nor winter
brittle cold, then damp
capable of harsh snowstorms
be thankful, November says

AR

while we were sleeping
this bit of magic happened:
the rain turned to snow.
it must have been beautiful
what we missed as we slumbered

AR

secrets in their house
really in the foundation
the couple shows up
wants therapeutic magic
all I can do is listen

GH

my sacred cocoon
the space in which I reside
to write, to create
other times it's my office
where people bring their anguish

GH

indoors many days
stepping outside is freedom
awakening air
to walk in the sun is bliss
to return home a blessing

AR

that lucky Snow White
one small bite of an apple
bought her a long nap
but I can't get any rest
till my emails are answered

KT

so many apples
sit with corn on the cob, squash,
heirloom tomatoes
they whisper: *we are the crops*
what you've all been waiting for

GH

narrowing options
aging has its challenges
(a euphemism)
what helps is being grateful
knowing youth was no picnic

GH

this image soothes me
they are swimming gracefully
loggerhead turtles
when asked why do you travel
it is to see this ballet

AR

words return as friends
after a prolonged absence
they come in, sit down
my heart swells, beating faster
please stay, it is whispering

AR

this sweet spongy soil
now opens itself to spring
turns to mud and sprout
invites the tired hungry geese
to gather and greet and graze

KT

enormous houses
so much money landscaping,
manicuring lawns;
I pass on my bicycle
to see wild turkeys gathered

AR

sleep-deprived first day
and then some insomnia
conclusion so far:
traveling is many things
but restful's not on the list

GH

still hot and humid
many are saying: *quiet!*
don't complain too much
winter will come soon enough
and my reply? *bring it on*

AR

procrastination
a form of self sabotage
one of so many
its cousins are denial
perseveration, pretense

GH

Hay(na)ku

3 lines
words: 1 - 2 - 3

fried
green tomatoes
taste like contentment

KT

cat
reminds me:
feed the birds

AR

tragedy
downgraded to
an unfortunate occurrence

GH

I
wonder about
Barack Obama's dreams

GH

it's
not about
what it's about

GH

morning
has arrived
daily so far

one
simple fact
to count on

                    KT

winter
only snowblowers
interrupt snow's peace
                    GH

peace
is found
on a bike

                    AR

men
old white ones
running the country
                    GH

walking
praising this
gift of motion

KT

men
at microphones
disgorging with pride

politicians
reveal themselves
by tone alone

KT

comfortable
flannel shirts
my winter uniform

GH

poems
are peanuts
I keep eating

KT

no
essential word
so often avoided

GH

192

conversation
so much
is not said

AR

peace
I watch
a turtle swim

AR

dreams
rich full
escape at dawn

KT

weep
again for
dead black men

KT

leaves
nearly gone
tree doesn't mind

she
stands ready
for winter's lesson

KT

travel
a noun
and a verb

GH

breeze
rustling leaves
green spirit song

KT

boys
racing bikes
summer's freedom fading

KT

nouns
need verbs
to get moving

GH

metaphor
my favorite
figure of speech

GH

aging
is like
a dripping faucet

GH

from
my wounds
the dead bleed

KT

peonies
open wide
life in pink

AR

change
a constant
not tolerated well

AR

please
be still
breathe: in, out

AR

preparing
for what
I don't know

AR

happy
valentine's day
I tell myself

GH

sleep
every night
plunging into mystery

KT

heaven
on earth:
the ordinary day

GH

ambiguity
it's neither
here nor there

GH

judgement
and comparison
the twin toxins

AR

determination
without it
nothing will happen

GH

petal
gentle wind
and you fall

AR

ice
like glass
hip fracture weather

GH

remember:
everything is
food for thought

GH

grief
accepting loss
rolling with it

GH

lost
internal compass
is not working

AR

grief
settles in
brings a suitcase

AR

coffee
dark elixir
you bring joy

AR

beautiful
half-moon
in morning sky

AR

grateful
for gratitude:
thank you squared

GH

veteran's
glove drawer
all left hands

KT

authenticity
is why
I love animals

GH

early
the snow
quiets the world

AR

life
is practice
like playing scales

AR

flowers
in winter
they are anti-depressants

GH

COVID 19

5 lines

19 syllables: 5 - 5 - 4 - 3 - 2

lines: double-spaced

(in honor of social distancing)

it's like bad weather

the way it unites

virus versus

all of us

worldwide

GH

for decades, threats of

viral pandemics

how is it then

we are not

prepared?

AR

I am reminded

of how sad I was

when I lost him

ev'ryday

there's grief

GH

Mike Pence, listen up:

if Jesus returned

in this crisis

he would wear

a mask

AR

shall we list ways to

be frugal with our

toilet paper

or shall we

resist

KT

no intimacy

can be possible

on a Zoom call

too awkward

oh well

GH

paranoia rules

OCD works well

mental illness

becoming

normal

GH

now I have crushes

on many store clerks

also on three

governors

of states

KT

let's be sure we mock

the hype, but not the

scary nature

of COVID-

19

GH

dream of a vaccine

that protects us from

the virus and

makes us less

stupid

AR

virtual vista

leaves me longing for

what we once had —

better than

nothing

AR

relaxed and relieved

robins chat all day

using only

their indoor

voices

KT

no longer immune

to our clueless ways

face-to-face now

fragile truth

appears

GH

pandemic birthdays

just nod when they come

know you're alive

wash your hands

be done

GH

now I realize

what I should have learned,

a life lesson:

how to cut

my hair

AR

here's what can happen

when health policies

are gutted by

corporate

money

KT

what I am missing:

spontaneity

going somewhere

just because

no mask

AR

now just two outfits

one for outdoors and

one for indoors

laundry is

easy

KT

unrelenting news

each day it gets worse

lungs, liver, brains

COVID's goal

pillage

GH

when the world resumes

the introverts will

feel gratitude

and also

sadness

KT

213

Pandemic Poems

Short-form poems written in response
to the COVID-19 pandemic

it's always about
doing the best you know how
adapting to change

we must keep living
while always being prudent
in the face of fear

this is not diff'rent
from normal life, except that
we're not distracted

by shopping, dining
drinking in public places
we are all holed up

what if people discovered
there is an inside life, too

GH ✦ Haiku Sonnet

my breath
fogs my glasses
caught underneath the mask;
and, sweating inside nitrile gloves,
my hands
keeping a safe distance, shopping,
nodding, acknowledging,
a smile lives in
the eyes

AR ✦ Butterfly Cinquain

in pandemic times
souls go delving and digging
old demons appear

someone famous wrote
that human evils arise
from our restlessness

we can't sit alone
in a room and bear our mind's
wild companionship

sadly for us all
this skill is not taught in school
and rarely in church

this is an Easter musing
about our need for saviors

KT ✦ Haiku Sonnet

I
wish I
liked to drink

GH ✦ Hay(na)ku

skin
like sandpaper
wash your hands

AR ✦ Hay(na)ku

OCD, hoarding
and even paranoia
are not disorders
in the midst of this crisis
practical adaptations

GH ✦ Tanka

ride
my bike
neck gaiter
at the ready

unmasked runners pant
bikers too, they huff and puff
gaiter up, I say *enough!*
I don't want your germs!

I dream the day
I go out
and just
ride

AR ✦ Arkquain

look! there! on my laptop screen — those are my loved
　　　ones
smiling, waving and speaking — or muting themselves
now they live as tiny squares — inside flattened rooms
being digitized, they say — *is strangely tiring*

KT ✦ Imayo

218

lungs
organ necessary for life
draws in air, expels carbon dioxide
gratitude
ventilator

GH ✦ Didactic Cinquain

phages are good viruses that help
by attacking bad viruses
so we don't need to freak out
about ev'ry virus
sometimes it's okay
we can relax
it might be
just a
phage

KT ✦ Nonet

maybe this pandemic is a chance
for people to think about life
and how they want to live it
let's all use the time well
social distancing
can still include
reaching out
loving
heart

GH ✦ Nonet

wild things
feeling safer
venture closer to town
coyotes, beaver, deer and owls
draw near
at the Mississippi shoreline
a single blue heron
stands relaxed on
one leg

KT ✦ Butterfly Cinquain

left
alone
in the house
43 days

how is this diff'rent
from what I would be doing
or what I'd be pursuing
if I could go out

my son visits
waves at me
I feel
left

GH ✦ Arkquain

psychotherapy by phone
a fair accommodation
no germs, no body language
just voices and love

GH ✦ Dodoitsu

all these dogs being walked at noontime
have a look of vague suspicion
that says *this is not normal*
what about 6 am
and then 5 pm?
they keep quiet
as they trot
gladly
on

KT ✦ Nonet

morning
through the window
there are birds unaware
of the limitations we have
six feet
means nothing to the cardinal
as he sings for his mate
she flies to him
freely

GH ✦ Butterfly Cinquain

times of extreme stress demand
we tap our deep resources
compassion, strength, love, humor
creativity

AR ✦ Dodoitsu

Costco
shoppers all
looking like bandits

AR ✦ Hay(na)ku

isolation
being separated from people
living apart
lonely
quarantine

GH ✦ Didactic Cinquain

wall
between
former life
and COVID world

when we're stuck at home
and we can't roam as before
we look around for a chore
and ponder the list

house clean, meals done
think I might
paint a
wall

KT ✦ Arkquain

no one told us it would be like this
enough time to hear your own voice
the unexpected pleasure
of amazing quiet
time spread out like sky
interruptions
disappear
mostly
calm

GH ✦ Nonet

a nation's crisis
unveiling
our inequities

KT ✦ Lune 1

ukelele
calls quietly
from its corner

now
no reason
not to answer

KT ✦ Hay(na)ku

hands
dirty
full of germs
we're now aware

of how to wash them:
use pure soap, liquid or bar
nothing obscure or bizarre
scrub fingers and thumbs

sing a short song
while you scrub
your two
hands

GH ✦ Arkquain

connections, produced by Zoom — who are we kidding
they are ways to stay in touch — such weak surrogates
watching the Travel channel — not like being there
the South of France on our screens — can't smell
    lavender

GH ✦ Imayo

now
people
shun the ones
who don't feel well

our trust is tested
in so many directions
we're wary of infections
and suspect the worst

someday we'll see
what's opaque
and dim
now

KT ✦ Arkquain

the extroverts are going crazy
their need to talk, converse, gather
they pursue repairmen and
innocent bystanders
with *how's it going?*
beautiful day!
pandemic
torture
rules

GH ✦ Nonet

inside
alone, quiet
an introvert's heaven
except it might last a long time
crisis

GH ✦ Cinquain

Constitution
once mighty
has been shredded

AR ✦ Hay(na)ku

sneezing
possible mechanism
to cause death

GH ✦ Hay(na)ku

stop
listen
there are birds
singing their hymns

a voice can be heard:
god, you kids. I need a rest
don't forget — Mother knows best.
sit there quietly

Earth repairing
it does that
if we
stop

AR ✦ Arkquain

I'm getting used to this quarantine
and in fact, I think I'll miss it
soon we'll be told to resume
and I can only hope
we will remember
the calm quiet
the kindness
the smiles
space

GH ✦ Nonet

sun rises and sets
unknown: who has the virus
we take precautions

restaurants become
creative during this time
curbside carry-out

but so-called leaders
standing in a group of twelve
tell us to distance

be compassionate
extroverts are panicking
so sad to witness

stay informed and wash our hands
breathe in and out, wash our hands

AR ✦ Haiku Sonnet

what do I do with my itch — the one on my nose
I don't dare use my own hands — but unless I find
a safe object for scratching — I might lose my mind
too attentive to instincts — what a disorder!

GH ✦ Imayo

down on Folwell Street
the red car in the driveway
has its doors open

couples and their kids
cross their yards toward the car
some dogs tag along

at 5:56
the car radio booms out
what we've waited for

sometimes in our lives
we all have pain and sorrow
sing it, Bill Withers

lean on me when you're not strong
our voices bridge the distance

KT ✦ Haiku Sonnet

flu
shortened
nickname for
influenza

like Lou for Louis
U.S. for United States
or b.p.m. for heart rate
abbreviated

don't waste your breath
if you're sick
with the
flu

GH ✦ Arkquain

my friends
make pretty masks
the fabric soft, bright, fun
and when I place it on my face,
there's love

AR ✦ Cinquain

what I have come to understand is:
the virus is not the problem
panic, fear, and most of all
a lack of leadership
now, there's your problem
for now, stay calm
wash your hands
and then
vote

AR ✦ Nonet

those are two right hands
in Rodin's famous sculpture,
so nearly touching
what has looked like tenderness
in these days looks like danger

KT ✦ Tanka

another virus
lives, spreads; it's
called anxiety

AR ✦ Lune 1

spring's the season for romance
also boredom or divorce
all options on the table
in pandemic times

KT ✦ Dodoitsu

fear, the tip of the iceberg — this plague brings lessons
struggles do not disappear — they don't die from this
a mind, body, spirit thing — now no distractions
before, during, and after — it's all the present

AR ✦ Imayo

thousands of Zoom groups
springing up
like dandelions

we prove once again
an old truth:
we're born to connect

KT ✦ Lune 1

wash hands
with awareness
soap is a miracle
mindful now of what has been touched
by whom
from the outside, bags and boxes;
as for other humans
eye contact, smiles
connect

AR ✦ Butterfly Cinquain

balloons like enormous Christmas lights
decorate a small front yard tree
there is more than one way to
celebrate, to connect;
video chatting
window singing
all good but
I miss
hugs

AR ✦ Nonet

we say
"flatten the curve"
the mantra of our times
in ominous or offhand tones
spoken

KT ✦ Cinquain

Poems About Poems

Poems written about the forms themselves

oh, Haiku Sonnet
you have come around again
I'm drawing a blank

what can I give you?
my cat, an easy subject
but he is idle

I've not one more word
to say about this virus,
the damage it's done

spring is beautiful
trees, flowers, whole blooming world
blah, blah, blah, blah, blah

oh thank god, the last two lines
see you next time. there! I'm done

AR

each line's shorter than the one before
and so the Nonet poem form
gradually takes the shape
of a short slant arrow
and then the last word
which is the last
line becomes
the main
point

KT

236

Shadorma
it could be some food
Greek menu
with grape leaves
delicious with lamb, feta
and baba ganoush

GH

incorrect Lune 2
a tiny mutant, a Lunatic
I take responsibility

GH

this poem form reminds me — of E. Dickinson
the squarish shape, the dashes — invite pensiveness
yet the way it spells and sounds — makes me want to
    say
I'll have turkey on whole grain — hold the imayo

KT

I'm partial
to this short-form one,
shadorma
who knows why
say it out loud: *Shadorma!*
it will make you smile

GH

"really" — "everything" —
are how many syllables?
it's not always clear

English is funny
even a word like "poem" —
it's not "pome" — is it?

it's no breeze for this
English-only verse writer
to get the forms right

how 'bout other tongues?
in Finnish there's no problem
syllables are math

the word "about" — forgive me —
I was forced to shorten it

                                        KT

Shadorma
I skipped over you
so sorry
no offense
it was not intentional
minor disorder

                                        AR

238

the Haiku Sonnet
is, for me, the toughest form
I rather dread it

inevitably
when it comes around again
I slap my forehead

a sonnet without
iambic pentameter?
are you kidding me?

and so I whine on
listing my sonnet complaints
in syllabic style

till this poem lives
in spite of myself

KT

sometimes
six words
make a poem

sometimes
six chairs
make a home

sometimes
six loves
make a life

KT

Shadorma!
these short-form poems
like caffeine
start my day
by waking up the right side
of my sleepy brain

GH

twenty minutes pass
not sure what to write about
there's always autumn,
the cat, time — or lack of it
voilá, well ... here's a Tanka

AR

a late night Lune 1
near bedtime
counting syllables

GH

poems
I love
shorter, the better

AR

More Said

(about the authors)

Gail Hartman
A POETIC RESUMÉ

1. I was born in a city of 8 million people called New York. It was crowded and vertical. My hometown newspaper was the *New York Times*.

2. In the year of my birth, the State of Israel was created. Ronald Reagan divorced his first wife, Jane Wyman. Gandhi was assassinated in New Delhi. Alfred Kinsey issued a revolutionary report on *The Sexual Behavior of the Human Male*. Tennessee Williams won a Pulitzer Prize for *A Streetcar Named Desire*. Babe Ruth died, as did Orville Wright. And a first-class postage stamp cost 3 cents.

3. My parents stayed very busy making their mark. My mother saw to it that some good books were published. My father made house calls and paid attention to the hearts of other people.

4. I went to a small all-girls school. I was 18 the first time I met a boy. To tell you the truth, it was anticlimactic, but still pleasant.

5. I made a four-year calendar by hand when I was 14, so that I could mark off the days one by one, until I could get out of the city. While my younger sister loved New York, I hated its loneliness, its crowds, its prohibitions: don't touch, don't talk to strangers, don't cross the street. Danger was lurking everywhere. And 9/11 was 40 years away.

6. I learned some important things in New York: money and happiness have no relationship with one another; ethnocentrism can be a form of prejudice; and psychotherapy is the greatest way to journey inward.

7. I escaped finally to a college in Ohio. This was farther west than anyone in my family had ever gone. My parents feared for me.

8. I loved Ohio. I loved how green it was and how the houses had roofs like triangles, not the flat-line ones of New York. I loved the passion of the antiwar demonstrators. I learned I was a part of an incredible generation. I belonged somewhere.

9. In college, I learned about art history, French literature, creative writing and sex.

10. I moved to our nation's capitol for a year, married to a nice man. We had two nice cats. I worked at a magazine called *National Geographic* and I was miserable. I hated the East Coast. I had to get out. Again.

11. We moved to North Dakota, which I know sounds dramatic. It was. My parents almost called the police. There are so many ways to rebel.

12. I fell in love with North Dakota: the flat mustard fields, the summer swimming holes, the adventure of living in a place that was totally foreign to me. I had never heard of the places I discovered: Minot, Manvel, Devils Lake, Durbin, Bisbee, Buxton. The map was like a poem.

13. My marriage was not like a poem, so it ended. He moved to the East Coast and I stayed for six more winters, to be exact. In those years, I found myself. A girl from Manhattan finds out who she is in Grand Forks, North Dakota. Almost a tabloid headline.

14. But just listen to the wealth I acquired in North Dakota: I became a potter; I taught braille; I collected stamps (but only pretty ones); I planted vegetables; I discovered, while driving due south to Fargo at dawn, that the sun rises in the east and sets in the west — which we had only heard about in New York. I studied psychology. I also met and married the love of my life.

15. He and I left North Dakota and moved next door to Minnesota. Years and years of making a household or two, making a baby or two, raising these babies, working at jobs I have loved: at a bookstore, at a radio station, and finally practicing psychotherapy.

16. Illness came into our Minnesota house, but then recovery, for a time, did, too. We learned to replace fear with hope, although I never got very good at it. When I drive by a hospital now, I look up and wish all the patients freedom from pain and waiting.

17. In New York, my father died at some point. A bittersweet loss. We spread his ashes in the Atlantic Ocean. My mother knew he hated sand, but oh well.

18. The children left home. I cried for years. I missed my son as though something in my soul had been amputated. But now I have become accustomed to the quiet. New York is very far away. I almost never go there. I prefer this place, with its magical storms, its grain elevators downtown, its lakes and even its limitations, none of which I can think of at the moment.

19. My husband died at the age of 62. We knew it was coming, but that did not lessen the agony. Eventually we lose everyone we love or they lose us. No way around that one. I discovered the miracle of resilience and the transformative power of deep grief.

20. Not much time left for me: with good luck, 20 more winters and 20 more gardens. At the beginning, they don't tell you what matters most: one beautiful ordinary day after another in a place you feel is home.

www.gailhartmanwriter.com

Ann Reed

Singer/songwriter Ann Reed has been performing for more than forty years with her rich, dark chocolate voice and songs that find a permanent place in the heart. Her ability to tell a story came from the Paying-Your-Dues part of her career. She was in a duo with another woman and both of them played the 12-string guitar. While her singing partner tuned, Ann told stories from the road. She knew that if she could reach a slightly tipsy (or in some cases completely inebriated) audience, the reaction from a receptive sober group of people would be amazing!

But this is a poetry book so here's the tie-in: as an adolescent, Ann Reed was saved by three things: the guitar, being funny, and poetry. She had the good fortune to end up in an experimental program in high school where she was allowed to explore all of these creative outlets and then some. The poems morphed into songs; the songs, humor and storytelling led to a successful career. Simple, right? Well, no. There is a fair amount of resilience and perseverance involved in the story but we are almost out of room.

Along with a catalog of hundreds of songs, Ann Reed is the author of a novel, *Citizens of Campbell.* She lives in Minneapolis, Minnesota with her wife and their cat, Momo.

www.annreed.com

Kate Tucker

Kate Tucker grew up in Decatur, Illinois, and spent some years studying literature and theater (Earlham College and University of Minnesota) before she found her way to seminary (Claremont School of Theology, Claremont, California and Earlham School of Religion). She served as Associate Minister at First Universalist Church, Minneapolis until she retired as Minister Emerita. Kate now writes, serves as a spiritual director, and remains involved with collegial projects in the Twin Cities. She has special affection for the farmlands of the Midwest, the deserts of Arizona, the mystery of creativity, and the unique stories that are our lives.

This little book combines three things Kate prizes: the nourishment of friendship, the power of words, and the fruitfulness of a daily practice — even a miniature practice that captures a moment by counting its syllables. These things together — friendship, words and commitment to a practice — create a sturdy scaffold for truthfulness, discovery and delight.

CPSIA information can be obtained
at www.ICGtesting.com
Printed in the USA
LVHW081929221120
672389LV00046B/493